D1275527

ECONOMY IN ACTION!

EYE ON ECONOMICS

Tamara L. Britton
ABDO Publishing Company

visit us at
www.abdopublishing.com

Printed in the United States of America, North Mankato, Minnesota.
052012
092012

 PRINTED ON RECYCLED PAPER

Cover Photo: Thinkstock
Interior Photos: Alamy p. 15; AP Images pp. 9, 17, 19, 21; iStockphoto pp. 1, 5, 6, 7, 10, 13, 25, 27; The United States Navy p. 11

Editors: Tamara L. Britton, Stephanie Hedlund
Art Direction: Neil Klinepier

Library of Congress Cataloging-in-Publication Data

Britton, Tamara L., 1963-
 Eye on economics / Tamara L. Britton.
    p. cm. -- (Economy in action!)
 ISBN 978-1-61783-487-5
 1. Economics--Juvenile literature. I. Title.
 HB183.B75 2013
 330--dc23
                              2012019053

Contents

What Is Economics?

Have you recently received money for your birthday? If so, you may have a list of gifts you would like to buy. Your list might include a tablet computer, skinny jeans, and a game system.

Your list has much to choose from! It would be great if you had enough money for everything. But you do not. So, which will you choose?

Such choices are the basis of economics. Economics is a science. It looks at how people use limited **resources** to satisfy unlimited needs and wants.

Seems simple, right? Well, it can be more **complex**. You see, people are not the only ones who make these decisions. Businesses, states, and countries do too. All these decisions and their effects create the economy.

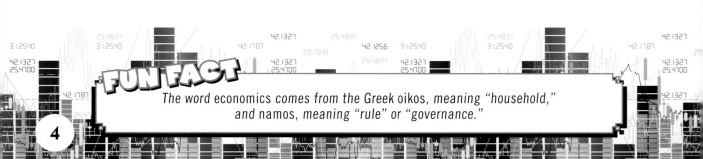

FUN FACT

The word economics comes from the Greek oikos, meaning "household," and namos, meaning "rule" or "governance."

When you spend your resources on goods you want, you are part of the economy!

Decisions, Decisions

Let's say you want a new tablet computer. To reach this goal, you worked all summer long. You also saved your allowance. Now, you look at your savings account record. One thousand dollars! You finally have enough to make your purchase.

When choosing between many things, a list of pros and cons can help you make the best decision.

One thousand dollars is a lot of money. Think of all the things you could buy! You can probably think of more than a thousand dollars worth. A new bike would be nice. So would some new clothes.

IT ALL ADDS UP!
Unlimited Wants + Limited Resources = Scarcity

Though you have one thousand dollars, your money is limited compared to your wants. So, you must choose between the tablet, the bike, or the clothes. You decide to stick with your original plan.

If you work hard and save the money you earn, you will be able to satisfy your needs and wants.

Economy Up Close

When you go to buy your tablet, the store is busy. Customers are trying out new products. They are also buying services such as memory upgrades.

The store's employees help the customers. The store pays them money for their labor. They spend their wages on goods and services from other businesses.

When **demand** for goods and services increases, businesses hire more employees. So, more people have money to spend. This is how the economy grows.

Tablets are very popular. So, the manufacturer supplied the market with enough to satisfy demand. **Supply** and demand decide what goods and services are available. They also decide cost. Prices rise when demand is greater than supply. Prices decrease if supply passes demand.

Okay, you know how individuals and businesses make decisions. You've seen the relationship between supply, demand, and price. All of these are **microeconomic** factors. Now let's take a look at the bigger picture.

In the first three months of 2012, the top five tablet companies shipped 17.1 million units! Apple led the way with more than 62 percent of the market.

Big Picture Economics

Did you wonder who made your tablet? Where it came from? How it got to you? These decisions take place in the macro economy.

Macroeconomics focuses on the total economy. It is concerned with factors such as **unemployment**, gross domestic product (GDP), and **inflation**.

Countries receive income from taxes. Sometimes they borrow money too. But like people and businesses, countries have limited **resources**. They also have unlimited needs and wants. So, they also must manage **scarcity**.

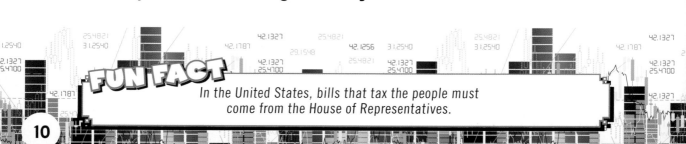

FUN FACT

In the United States, bills that tax the people must come from the House of Representatives.

While we choose between tablets, bikes, and clothes, a government's choices have a greater impact. They must choose between aircraft carriers and health care funding.

World Economies

Different countries use different economic systems. In free market economies, private decision makers decide how **resources** are used. Means of production such as factories, farms, and mines are privately owned. Businesses buy resources to produce goods and services. People sell their labor to earn money. **Supply** and **demand** determine prices of goods and services.

In a managed economy, central planners make most major economic decisions. The public or state owns the means of production. Planners decide what to produce, who to hire, and how much to pay. They decide where to sell goods and services. They also decide what those things will cost.

In a mixed economy, markets decide how resources are used. They also decide what goods and services are produced, how they are **distributed**, and who receives them. But in some industries, the government makes these decisions.

Governments, businesses, and people make many economic decisions between producing a tablet and distributing it to you.

13

International Trade

No matter their economic system, nations trade with each other. They produce different goods and services. Each **specializes** in goods they have the **resources** to produce.

For example, Saudi Arabia produces oil. The United States produces wheat. Argentina produces beef. Even tiny countries have something to trade. Sri Lanka produces cinnamon!

If you check out your new tablet, you can see which country made it. Let's say your tablet was built in China. The government imported parts to build it. Manufacturers paid for labor to assemble it. Finally, the tablet was exported from China and imported where you live!

MAJOR INTERNATIONAL TRADING PARTNERS

US: China, Canada, Mexico, Japan
CANADA: US, China, United Kingdom, Mexico
MEXICO: US, China, Canada, South Korea

The United States is the world's largest exporter of wheat.

Imports and Exports

Exports are goods produced in one country then shipped to another for sale or trade. Exports help a country's economy expand by selling more than its population can buy. So, exports can create jobs.

When an export reaches its destination, it becomes an import. Imports are goods that are not produced locally. They can be similar to local goods. In that case, the imports are lower in price or better in quality. This causes local producers to improve products to compete.

What a great deal, right? Each nation produces what it has **resources** for. Then, they trade with each other. If a country exports more than it imports, it has a trade **surplus**. But sometimes a country imports more than it exports. Then it has a trade **deficit**.

MAJOR NORTH AMERICAN PORTS

US: Ports of Los Angeles and Long Beach, CA; Port of New York and New Jersey; Port of South Louisiana, LA; Port of Houston, TX

CANADA: Port Metro Vancouver, BC; Port of Montréal, QC

MEXICO: Port of Manzanillo, CL; Ports of Veracruz, Tuxpan, and Coatzacoalcos, VE; Port of Tampico, TM

China's Port of Shanghai is the world's busiest port.

Trade Barriers

A trade **deficit** can slow a nation's economy. For example, a nation with a trade deficit spends more than it earns. To avoid this, governments often make rules against the movement of goods between countries. These are called trade **barriers**.

Trade barriers can solve other problems too. Sometimes local businesses can't compete with those in other countries. Import **restrictions** can remove foreign competition.

Lowering import restrictions can open new markets. This can promote economic growth. However, restricting imports can protect a nation's producers from being forced out of business by lower-cost goods.

Trade barriers make goods cost more. So they eliminate the benefit of producing goods at the most **efficient** cost. In addition, they make it difficult for nations to sell their products. So they take away the benefit of **specialization**.

In 2011, the United States had a $282 billion trade deficit with China. The US has placed tariffs on some Chinese imports, such as tires.

Trade Agreements

Sometimes, countries want to trade without **barriers**. They believe free trade will improve their economies. So, they make agreements among themselves.

Trade agreements end tariffs and other **restrictions** among member nations. They also allow workers and **assets** to move freely across borders.

The European Union (EU) began in 1993. It has 27 member nations. They work together as a single market. They operate as one economic unit.

Canada, the United States, and Mexico are members of the North American Free Trade Agreement (NAFTA). NAFTA went into effect January 1, 1994. It eliminated trade barriers between its member nations.

The World Trade Organization (WTO) was created in 1995. It helps its 155 member nations with international business. It oversees international trade agreements.

Trade agreements do not always benefit everyone. Some Mexican corn farmers cannot compete with lower-priced corn imported from the United States. So, they cannot afford to continue farming their land.

Economic Indicators

So now you know a little more about **macroeconomics**! You may be wondering what the goal of all this is. Well, nations make decisions so that their economies will grow.

How do officials know if an economy is healthy? They study economic indicators. These include the gross domestic product (GDP), the consumer price index (CPI), and the **unemployment** rate.

A country's GDP is the value of all the goods and services it produces. It is counted during a certain amount of time. In a healthy economy, the GDP grows.

The CPI looks at the total cost of a number of goods. It is also counted over time. In a healthy economy, the CPI is stable.

In any economy there are people who are willing and able to work. Yet some do not have jobs. The count of these people is the unemployment rate.

FUN FACT

Full Employment and Balanced Growth Act of 1978 set an unemployment goal of four percent of workers age 16 and older.

GROSS DOMESTIC PRODUCTS

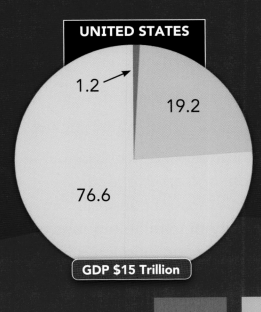

UNITED STATES

1.2
19.2
76.6

GDP $15 Trillion

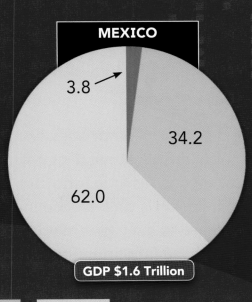

MEXICO

3.8
34.2
62.0

GDP $1.6 Trillion

Agriculture | Industry | Service

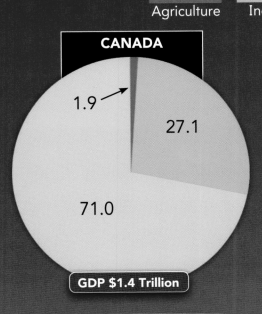

CANADA

1.9
27.1
71.0

GDP $1.4 Trillion

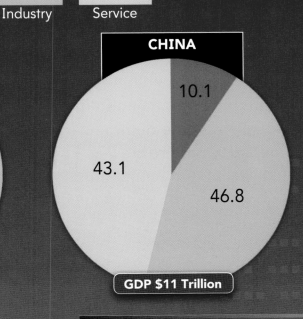

CHINA

10.1
46.8
43.1

GDP $11 Trillion

Boom or Bust?

What happens if a nation's economy does not grow? What if it contracts? Sometimes, economic conditions result in **inflation**, **deflation**, and stagflation.

Inflation is an increase in prices. This may be caused by an increase in the money **supply**. A **scarcity** of available goods can also cause inflation. Stagflation happens when inflation is high, and the **unemployment** rate is high too.

People who are unemployed may not have any income. They may not want to spend their savings. This can cause a **surplus** of available goods. Too many available goods can cause prices to deflate.

IT ALL ADDS UP!

Reduced Economic Activity + Increased Unemployment = Recession

Contracting GDP + High Unemployment + Time = Depression

Foreclosures at

Bank Owned Property
Call for Special Financing Options
on this Bank Owned Property
24 Hour FREE
Recorded Message
CALL NOW!

In 2007, the Great Recession began. By 2010, the unemployment rate was more than nine percent. Millions of people could not make their house payments and lost their homes.

One World Nation

The world's population continues to increase. If a country's economy does not grow, its **standard of living** will decrease. So, governments carefully watch economic indicators. They work to keep their economies in **equilibrium**.

Today, we are part of a global village. An import **duty** on wheat in China can mean less income for the United States. An increase in oil exports in Saudi Arabia can mean lower gasoline prices in France.

It is important for nations to understand their economic decisions affect all the world's people. So let's all keep our eye on economics!

ECON EXAM

The United States produces 22 billion pounds (10 billion kg) of rice each year. If an importer wants to import brown basmati rice, the federal government charges $0.0413 for each kilogram (2.2 lbs). This is an example of:

a) a trade agreement
b) a trade barrier

c) an import quota
d) none of the above

Answer Key: b

For the winter of 2011-2012, a sporting goods store in Minnesota stocked up on snow boots. But that winter was the fourth warmest on record! Few customers bought snow boots. What would be the result of this?

a) low demand for snow boots caused the store to lower the price

b) other stores lowered the price of their snow boots to remain competitive

c) money lost on snow boot sales reduced each store's profits

d) all of the above

Answer Key: d

EXPORT MATCH

You may be familiar with common countries and their exports. But smaller countries also trade. Match each country with its chief export:

1. Bhutan	a. minerals
2. Brunei	b. clothing
3. Burkina Faso	c. cotton
4. Cambodia	d. food products
5. Estonia	e. electricity
6. Eritrea	f. gold
7. Kyrgyzstan	g. crude oil and natural gas
8. Latvia	h. livestock
9. North Korea	i. machinery and electrical equipment
10. Togo	

Answer Key:
1) e 2) g 3) f 4) b 5) i 6) h 7) f 8) d 9) a 10) c

Glossary

asset - something of value owned by a person, a business, or a government.

barrier - a law or rule that makes something difficult or impossible.

complex - having many parts, details, ideas, or functions.

deficit - an amount that is less than the amount that is needed.

deflation - a decrease in the price of goods and services.

demand - the amount of an available product that buyers are willing and able to purchase.

distribute - to give out or deliver something to each individual in a group.

duty - a tax on goods that are being brought into a country.

efficient - wasting little time or energy.

equilibrium - a state in which opposing forces are balanced.

inflation - a rise in the price of goods and services.

macroeconomics - the study of the whole economy.

microeconomics - the study of the market behavior of people and businesses.

resources - something that can be used to increase wealth.

restrict - to keep within certain limits.

scarce (SKEHRS) - an amount less than what is needed.

specialize - to limit business to a specific area.

standard of living - the amount of wealth, comfort, and possessions that a person or group has.

supply - the amount of something available for sale.

surplus - an amount above what is needed.

unemployment - the state of being out of work. Someone who is out of work is unemployed.

Web Sites

To learn more about the economy in action, visit ABDO Publishing Company online. Web sites about economics are featured on our Book Links page. These links are routinely monitored and updated to provide the most current information available.

www.abdopublishing.com

Index